918.66 Perry, Roger
PER
        The Galapagos
        Islands

DATE			

© THE BAKER & TAYLOR CO.

The Galápagos Islands

The Galápagos Islands

by Roger Perry

ILLUSTRATED WITH PHOTOGRAPHS AND A MAP

DODD, MEAD & COMPANY · NEW YORK

CREDITS: Paul Colinvaux, 16-17; Tjitte de Vries, 10, 12, 15, 19, 23, 27, 32, 33, 37, 39, 41, 47, 56, 58, 60, 61, 65, 73, 74, 76, 79, 84; Sven Gillsäter, 80; Roger Perry, 2, 11, 18, 25, 26, 28, 30, 31, 42, 44, 48-49, 53, 54, 59, 63, 69, 81, 88, 89; Rolf-Dieter Sievers, 86; Daniel Weber, 67.

Map by Salem Tamer

Frontispiece: The marine iguana is near to the legendary dragon in appearance.

ACKNOWLEDGMENTS

I would like to express my gratitude to Mr. G. T. Corley Smith and Mr. P. J. Hobbs for their help in various ways with the preparation of this book; Mr. Jacob Lundh and Sr. Jacinto Gordillo, for information about the early settlement of the islands; Dr. Keith Howard, of the U. S. Geological Survey, for telling me about volcanoes; Dr. Paul Colinvaux, Mr. Sven Gillsäter, Mr. Rolf-Dieter Sievers, and Mr. Daniel Weber, for kindly allowing me to use their photographs; and, above all, Dr. Tjitte de Vries, of Amsterdam University, for the use of many photographs and his helpful criticisms. I am especially appreciative to Miss Dorothy Bryan for her editorial advice. To all these go my deepest thanks.

Contents

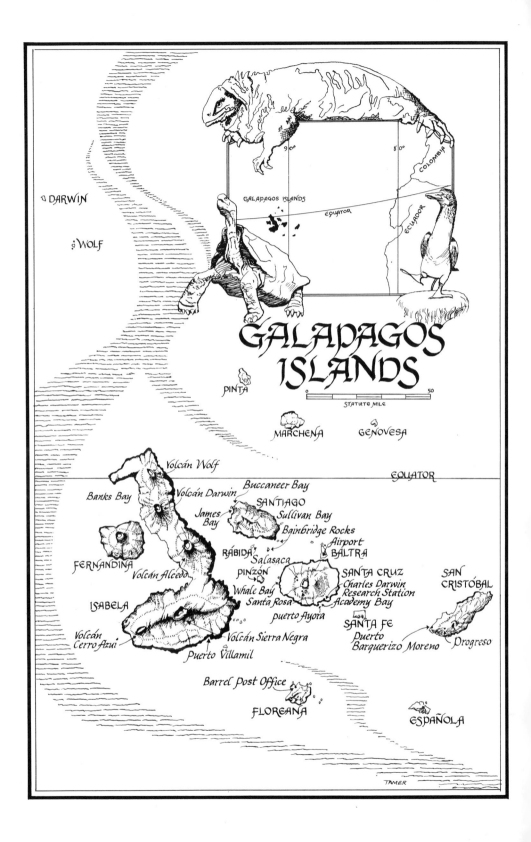

GALAPAGOS ISLANDS

9'00 8'00

COLOMBIA

DARWIN

WOLF

GALAPAGOS ISLANDS

EQUATOR

ECUADOR

GALAPAGOS ISLANDS

PINTA

0   STATUTE MILE   50

MARCHENA   GENOVESA

Volcán Wolf   EQUATOR

Banks Bay   Volcán Darwin   Buccaneer Bay
                                        SANTIAGO
                        James   Sullivan Bay
                        Bay   Bainbridge Rocks
                                             Airport
                        RÁBIDA   BALTRA
FERNANDINA   Salasaca
                   PINZÓN
Volcán Alcedo   SANTA CRUZ   SAN
                   Whale Bay   Charles Darwin   CRISTÓBAL
ISABELA   Santa Rosa   Research Station
                                        Academy Bay
                          puerto Ayora SANTA FE
Volcán   Puerto
Cerro Azul   Volcán Sierra Negra Barquerizo Moreno   Progreso
         Puerto Villamil

                   Barrel Post Office

                   FLOREANA   ESPAÑOLA

TAMER

1

Land of Volcanoes

Far out into the equatorial waters of the eastern Pacific, the sea breaks against the cliffs of a group of lonely islands. These are the Galápagos, an eerie and strangely forbidding part of the world, where miniature moonscapes studded with cactus trees and black rocks rise darkly from the ocean. Hordes of dragonlike iguanas cluster along the shores and somehow bring to mind the dawn of a prehistoric era when life first came on to land. Here also live huge, lumbering tortoises, coral red crabs, penguins, and a host of strange creatures found nowhere else in the world. Renowned pirates and adventurers—men like William Dampier and Ambrose Cowley—came here to rest and provision their ships after raids along the Spanish coast of South America. No wonder these remote islands have come down through history shrouded in mystery and legend!

My first acquaintance with the Galápagos was one day in 1964. I had traveled there to join a team studying ways of setting up a national park and preserving for all time this strange wildlife. Among my earliest and most vivid impressions were those of hot and arid islands, twisted and broken by the forces of their volcanic origin, set in the calm of a blue equatorial sea.

Beauty rides the Beast—a mockingbird and a land iguana.

The Galápagos are the tops of huge volcanoes. Where they now rise there once stretched unbroken ocean. Then, gradually, over the course of time, molten lava began to well up through the ocean floor. The sea seethed and boiled as the volcanoes grew, eruption followed eruption, and islands were thrust, black and smoldering, above the surface of the water. Eventually, the summits of many different volcanoes appeared, the highest soaring to over five thousand feet above the level of the sea. Geologists believe that all this began a few million years ago, probably in an epoch known as the Pliocene. This was an important and, geologically speaking, recent period in the history of life, when most of the groups of mammals we know today were already spreading over the continental areas of the world.

The mainland of South America lies, at its nearest point, over five hundred miles to the east of the Galápagos. Today, the islands are a part of Ecuador, where they are known officially as the *Archipiélago de Colón* (Columbus' Archipelago). They form a rather scattered group of islands, straddling the equator, and stretching over 23,000 square miles of the eastern Pacific.

The largest island is Isabela, J-shaped, seventy miles long and forty across at its base. It is made up of a line of giant volcanoes, capped by wide summit craters and joined together on their flanks. Four other major islands, although far smaller

Stark volcanic scenery overlooking Sullivan Bay in the Galápagos Islands.

Bainbridge is a group of small rocky islets off the coast of Santiago. Flamingoes (seen at right) come to feed in the shallow waters of the crater lake in the foreground.

than Isabela, are over fifteen miles across. Three of these, Fernandina, Santa Cruz, and Santiago, are each built from a single large volcano, while on San Cristóbal several peaks and ridges are united by low-lying fields of lava. Eight smaller islands complete the principal group of the archipelago. But, besides these, there is a host of islets, rocks, and reefs, some little more than the remains of volcanic cones that have been worn and hollowed away by the sea. The total land area of the archipelago is some 3,028 square miles—just under half the size of the state of Hawaii.

Although the Galápagos have never been joined to the mainland of South America, it has long been suggested that they were not always quite as isolated as they are today. The Cocos Ridge runs under the sea and extends almost all the way from Costa Rica to the northern part of the archipelago. The island of Cocos itself rises as a peak on this ridge. Some biologists believe that this, and another submarine ridge which runs toward the coast of mainland Ecuador, may represent the remains of lands that once rose above the sea. Even though such earlier landmasses, serving as a series of steppingstones, would help to explain the origin of some of the life on the Galápagos Islands, there is still too little evidence to support or disprove their former existence. The only proof is likely to come after geophysicists and oceanographers have studied in detail the islands and surrounding ocean floor.

The story of the climate of the Galápagos begins in the faraway waters of the southern Pacific Ocean. Here, off the coast of Chile, is born the Humboldt (or Peru) Current. Flowing northward, it brings a cold stream along the coast of Peru, toward the equatorial regions of the Pacific. Somewhere off southern Ecuador, it turns northwestward and sweeps across to the Galápagos. From May to December, during the southeasterly trade wind period, the shores of the southern islands are bathed in these cool waters. The surface winds in turn are chilled and they bring strangely cool conditions for islands on the equator.

These months are normally the drier season of the year. Rains are scarce, and they fall mainly as a fine, misty drizzle. Generally, the coastal regions of these islands are too dry for plants to thrive, except such growths as lichens, some thorns, and cacti that can survive long, rainless periods. But higher up, on the southern slopes of the larger islands, clouds and mists are more frequent, and, there, the moisture is enough to support fairly dense vegetation. On the very tops, around the summits of San Cristóbal, Santa Cruz, and par-

13

ticularly on the volcanoes of Isabela, are stretches of open country, with grasses and brakes of fern.

The rainy season is variable, but in most years there are occasional showers from January to about the end of April. At the beginning of this moist period, the winds die down and shift gently to the northeast. The islands then come more under the influence of a warm sea current flowing to the south from the direction of Central America. This is the time of the doldrums, of long calms with little wind, when sailing ships of the past would drift for many days, entirely at the mercy of the currents. In such a calm as this, in March, 1535, the Spaniards first came to the Galápagos, carried away helplessly from the coast of South America, deep into the still unexplored Pacific. Yet, these early months of the year are a delightful time to be in the islands, for the days are warm and the seas have a look of glassy stillness. On the mountains above there may be heavy rains, and, for a while, there comes the welcome sight of water cascading down long-dry stream beds.

In certain years, this current from the north flows unusually far to the south. It displaces the Humboldt Current, and the changes it brings may have grave consequences on the minute, floating plants and animals of the sea. Over wide areas, along the coast of South America, this sometimes results in the death of large numbers of the fish and sea birds that are dependent on this small marine life for their food. Latin Americans call this warm current *El Niño* (meaning Holy Child) because its presence in these years is usually first felt around Christmastime.

On approaching the islands, one can see very quickly how these two features, the climatic setting and their volcanic origin, have dominated the Galápagos scene. The coastal lowlands are arid and made up of an undulating, jumbled terrain of broken lava, reddish-brown soil, and scattered

14

plants. The cacti are enormous—thirty feet high—and they tower above the dry and mostly gray, leafless scrub. Open spaces are mere wastelands of boulders, broken by volcanic cones and fissures and crossed here and there by great, frozen rivers of lava. Where these flows reach the sea, they end in low cliffs or small, jagged points of land, divided by little bays. In the more sheltered of these, where there are sandy beaches and lagoons among the lava, mangroves and a few other kinds of salt-water plants grow. From a long way off the coast, these spots stand out as strips of bright emerald green against the blue of the sea and the black lava shoreline.

Altogether, there are several thousand small craters and cones scattered over the archipelago. Many have broken down with time, while others look as fresh as if they had appeared only a few days before. Some of the more conspicuous are perched on peninsulas near the sea, or set like islands in flows

Lava flows on the lower slope of Cerro Azul on Isabela. The summit of this great volcano, over 5,000 feet high, is hidden in mist.

010167

of black lava. They are made up of cinder and brittle lava, some black, others reddish and daubed with black and taffy-colored streaks. They are a striking feature and give to the Galápagos the lunar quality of their landscapes, similar to those made so familiar to millions through the Apollo flights and the moon walks and rides of the astronauts.

Lava flows descend from many of these cones and from fissures on the sides of the volcanoes. On Isabela and Fernandina, long black fingers of lava make the mountains look like immense cauldrons that have boiled over at their sides. Some flows have a smooth surface, easy to walk upon, although they are humped and buckled by pressure ridges. Others, little more than jumbled blocks, are so unsteady and have such razor-sharp edges that they make traveling difficult and quite dangerous. Dating studies have shown that the majority of these lavas seen on the surface today came from eruptions within the last million years.

The summit craters of the great volcanoes of Isabela and Fernandina are huge, bowl-shaped depressions, each measuring from one to several miles across. They have been formed

Before the eruption of 1968, a lake partly covered the lava floor of the huge caldera of Fernandina. (The photographs appearing in this panorama of Fernandina were mounted by the Department of Photography, Ohio State University.)

by subsidence and are known as *calderas*. As lava flowed from cones and fissures on the flanks of these volcanoes during eruptions, large chambers were left behind, underground. The calderas were formed as the overlying crust collapsed and fell into these chambers. This may happen on a number of occasions, over long intervals of time, the floor of the depression growing deeper and deeper as one huge deposit of crust debris follows another.

On a still day in June, 1968, the Galápagos Islands were rocked by a tremendous explosion. Shortly afterward, a great mushroom-shaped cloud rose high into the sky and fine volcanic ash fell over a wide area of the archipelago. Although we did not know it at the time, this was the beginning of a huge collapse of the floor of the summit crater of Fernandina.

I had already climbed Fernandina several times over the previous three years. It is a fascinating place, not the least reason being the immense size of the volcano. Although rising a mile above the sea, it really stands three miles above the bed of the Pacific. The walls of the caldera are twelve miles around, and—before that fateful June day—they fell away for

Pintail ducks swimming on the crater lake before the great eruption

two thousand feet to a shimmering, green lake on the crater floor. In this unlikely, reed-fringed oasis lived a large number of Galápagos pintails. I had counted 1,929 of these ducks, that are peculiar to the archipelago, on a visit there earlier in 1968. Many other birds and a large colony of land iguanas also had their home in the heart of this remote island.

I determined to visit Fernandina again as soon as I could after the eruption, to see what had happened. Although six days elapsed before I reached the island, the floor of the caldera was still settling down, and, as it subsided, in a series of short drops, the whole volcano was being rocked in waves of quivering tremors. As a group of us climbed slowly to the lip of the summit crater, we were shaken many times by these tremors, and a few of them were so violent that it was difficult to keep our footing. When we reached the top, it was not possible to see far into the crater because of the continuous

18

Floor of the caldera of Cerro Azul. Black lava, from an eruption twenty or thirty years ago, has flowed partly around a large cone near the base of the wall.

rockfalls and clouds of dust. Hundreds of tons of rocks were avalanching down the inner walls of the caldera, and the sound that rose and fell after each tremor was like that of a giant cataract. Only later did we learn that the floor had fallen another twelve hundred feet and the lake—still miraculously intact—had shifted to one end. The ducks had vanished.

Five months after this, when all the turmoil had calmed, we climbed down the now over three-thousand-foot-inner wall of the Fernandina caldera to the new crater floor. Many ducks were again in the depression, and we could only hope that some of these at least were survivors that had escaped in time from the cataclysm.

The archipelago is regarded today as one of the world's largest and most active groups of oceanic volcanoes. There have been eruptions on six of the islands since the beginning of the nineteenth century. Unexpectedly, at the end of 1970, steam vents were found on Santa Fe—an island composed of blocks of what were originally submarine lavas and long supposed to have been inactive. But the most active volcanoes of the Galápagos today are the highest and most westerly, namely Isabela and Fernandina. It is on these two islands that all the eruptions of recent years have taken place.

2

The Flow of Life

As the volcanoes and great lava fields cooled and hardened, life came in one way and another to the Galápagos. Over hundreds of thousands of years, wind and water carried countless seeds, insects, and other animals out across the Pacific toward the islands. Most of these must have perished on the way or even after their arrival on these inhospitable shores. But over the centuries a few managed to establish themselves.

Marine plants and animals were among the first to arrive, finding refuge in the shallow seas sheltered by the islands. From time to time, various crustaceans, mangroves, and other species of shore life drifted along on the Humboldt Current. Sea birds came, attracted by the rich marine life, and some stayed and nested.

For many thousands of years only the hardiest of the early arrivals stood a chance of surviving in the harsh environment they encountered inland. Among the first would have been lichens and similar primitive plants that can germinate from minute spores carried by the wind. The lichens, which absorb moisture from the air, are peculiarly adapted to surviving in exposed places. They are among the first plants to grow on the raw, lava-strewn Galápagos wastelands and provide much of the color, the yellowy-greens and grays, that one notices in these areas when approaching the islands from the sea. Certain mosses settle very quickly on volcanic ash. This was demonstrated to me very clearly after the recent eruption on Fernandina; it was only a matter of months before mosses were established on the newly fallen ash. As the dry season came along, their colors turned and these little plants made the upper parts of the volcano look as if they had been dusted with carpets of richly golden bread crumbs.

Following the original simple plants, others arrived on the Galápagos—grasses, cacti, and shrubs. These provided food for insects and a few kinds of land birds and reptiles. We can only guess by what means many of these creatures reached the islands. Great rafts of floating vegetation were probably the means of transportation in a number of cases. During torrential rains and heavy flooding on the mainland, large tangled mats of debris are carried out to sea on the swollen rivers. Such floating islands, on which animal life could certainly be trapped, have been seen many miles from the coast of South America, drifting westward on the current. In as little as ten or twelve days, these rafts, with their involuntary passengers, could reach the Galápagos Islands. Winds brought along birds and insects. The birds deposited seeds and small invertebrates with their droppings or possibly adhering to their feet.

The Galápagos tortoises are presumably descended from ancestors that floated away accidentally from some mainland stock many hundreds of thousands of years ago and somehow managed to survive on the islands in which they were marooned. Although these giant tortoises reach enormous sizes in the course of their long lives—nobody knows quite how long they live—when they first hatch they are only two inches in length, so it is possible that young members of the species

22

The dome-shaped tortoise of Volcan Alcedo, on Isabela. The native Galápagos hawk finds a convenient lookout on the four-foot shell.

were transported originally on a raft of vegetation. Gradually, their descendants spread over the emerged lands of the Galápagos. Perhaps, once in a while, flows of molten lava trapped and forced individuals into the sea, where they drifted until they reached other islands.

Because of the difficulties and dangers of crossing the wide stretch of ocean separating the islands from the continent, the Galápagos have relatively few species of plants and animals. There are many significant absentees. Fresh-water animals, such as frogs, salamanders, mayflies, and caddis flies, could never survive the sea journey, and none of these are found in the islands. Apart from two species of bats, the only native land mammals are small, ratlike rodents.

The few successful colonists had, however, one great advantage—there was little competition from other species. Having the islands very much to themselves, they could, in the course of many generations, develop into a number of novel and peculiar forms to be found nowhere else in the world. As the Galápagos are not a single island, but a group, it was possible for one species to develop on lines not only different from those originally held on the mainland but they could also differ from one little island to another.

In the interiors of the islands, roaming to the very summits of the largest volcanoes, live the giant tortoises and the land iguanas. Both are vegetarian. In the absence of deer and similar mammals, it was these reptiles that became the dominant grazing and browsing animals on land. The tortoises in particular have flourished in the Galápagos, developing into giants weighing anywhere up to a quarter of a ton. When man first discovered the islands, there were hundreds of thousands of them. Owing to the ruthless way in which they were slaughtered, there are now only a few thousand left and some races have been exterminated altogether.

The land iguanas are yellowish and brown lizards that grow to be up to four feet in length. I have seen them only in the very barren regions, where they live on the sparse seasonal vegetation and fallen cactus fruits. In suitable areas, however, as among the cindery soils on the rims of the great craters, where they are able to dig their burrows, they may be quite abundant. During the day, when they are feeding and sunning themselves, it is often possible to walk up close to these large lizards. They shake their heads in a very threatening manner, but, if anyone approaches too near, their nerve suddenly gives way and they make an unceremonious dash for their holes. But they can be vicious and, if handled incautiously, will give a nasty bite. Like the tortoises, the land iguanas vary from island to island.

Lava lizards live on most of the main islands. These are a smaller type, scarcely a foot long, that dart among the rocks

The land iguana, which thrives on juicy cactus pads, swallowing the sharp spines whole, may weigh up to fifteen pounds.

in search of insects. They have been divided into seven different species, which differ from one another in size, in color, and in behavior. All these reptiles are endemic to the Galápagos, that is, they are species that are found nowhere else in the world.

As with the reptiles, so it is with the Galápagos insects: they are not found in such great variety as in the equatorial regions of the continent, but those groups that have established themselves in the archipelago have developed into a range of different forms. Among the more successful of these are the ants and certain beetles, such as the little darkling beetles that come out in the cool of the night. The insects—and also the spiders and the land snails—have adapted in many diverse and ingenious ways to survive in the harsh environment. Some live in lichens. Others make themselves silken shelters or draw together tiny canopies of leaves where they while away the hot hours of the day. There are several curious cactus-eating groups that tunnel into the fleshy pads of prickly pears. Two kinds of water beetles and several varieties of dragonfly nymphs thrive in the sulphurous waters that collect in basins high up on the volcanoes.

The majority of the plants are adapted in one way or another to the dry environment. There are woodlands in the Galápagos, but they occur mainly in moist and favorable situations on the slopes and higher parts of the largest islands. Even in these spots, lushness is seasonal. Moisture-loving mosses and ferns, and even a few orchids, that thrive after the rains, quickly die back as the dry season comes, managing to survive until the rains return.

Among the many plants unique to the archipelago, none is

Forest of prickly pear cacti are a common feature of the desertlike lowlands of the Galápagos.

The large yellow flowers of the prickly pear open at the beginning of the warm season.

more bizarre than the tree cactus with its reddish trunk as thick as that of a good-sized pine. It is really a giant form of prickly pear, with yellow waxy flowers, three to four inches across.

Scalesias are another very curious group. Related to the sunflower, but with small, whitish blooms, they have developed into a score of species, varying from island to island. Some are forty feet high, with slender trunks forming strange, sunflower tree forests; others are no more than low shrubs which make vivid patches of green among the lava fields of the coasts.

Most of the land birds are also peculiar to the islands. The most abundant are small, dusky-brown or blackish finches, with stumpy tails. Anywhere among the cactus forests no more characteristic sounds can be heard than the lisping and rather monotonous calls of these birds. They are known as Darwin's finches, because they provided the great scientist

The Galápagos woodpecker finch is one of the world's most extraordinary birds. Living the life of a woodpecker, but lacking that bird's long tongue, it has learned to use an implement to get its food.

with perhaps the most striking evidence for his theory of evolution. There are thirteen species, differing remarkably from each other in the size and shape of their beaks, and yet clearly descended from a common ancestral stock. From an original species they have "radiated" in different directions. In the absence of representatives of the majority of the familiar families of songbirds, these finches behave in the Galápagos like warblers, grosbeaks, tanagers, titmice, troupials, honeycreepers, and even woodpeckers! Their beaks vary from the slender, pointed bills of insect-eaters to the huge, thick beaks of the seed-eating finches. The woodpecker finch uses a small twig or cactus spine to probe insects from crevices in the bark of trees. This is one of the very rare instances of a bird using a tool. What is rarer still is that the woodpecker finch actually makes its tool, breaking the twig to the right size for the job in hand. Besides finches, the archipelago has several species of land birds found nowhere else, particularly mockingbirds.

But it is as a haven for sea birds that the Galápagos Islands are truly remarkable. To the shelter of their lonely shores come petrels, shearwaters, frigate and tropic birds, boobies, albatrosses, gulls, and terns. During the northern winter, countless thousands of migrant phalaropes from the United States and Canada fly to feed on the offshore waters. Waders from as far away as Alaska visit their beaches and lagoons. Even the bobolink and the barn swallow occasionally make the long journey.

The Galápagos are fortunate in having no less than three species of boobies, and the 140,000 pairs of red-footed boobies that nest among the dried scrub and sun-baked headlands of Genovesa probably form the largest breeding colony of this species in the world. In addition, large colonies of masked boobies, storm petrels, and frigate birds have turned this island into one huge, noisy citadel of sea birds.

What is most remarkable about the frigates or man-o'-war birds is the effortless ease with which they soar in the skies. Although they have a seven- or eight-foot wingspan, their lightly built bones do not weigh more than a quarter of a pound. This gives them a higher ratio of wing-surface to body weight than that of any other bird. They are the pirates of the Galápagos bird world and use their mastery of the air in pursuing boobies and other birds, terrorizing them into disgorging the fish they have caught, which the frigates then catch in the air with extraordinary skill. In their breeding colonies, they spend much of their time stealing one another's eggs and the sticks with which they build their nests. The male is all black but he has a tiny, crimson pouch in his throat which, when courting, he blows up into a balloon the size of a large grapefruit to attract passing females.

The red-footed booby lives on fish and nests in trees.

The male frigate bird puffs up its bright throat pouch to attract female attention during courtship.

Española is the home of the Galápagos or waved albatross. Every year, several thousands of these great, oceanic wanderers return to nest on this one waterless island. They do not alight on any other land in the world, not even on the other islands of the Galápagos. The first comers arrive by the end of March, and the females lay their single egg in May or June. It takes the parents a long time to rear their enormous chick and it is a full six months before the family is ready to leave Española and range far over the tropical Pacific.

Even more curious birds that are to be seen on the archipelago are the flightless cormorant and the Galápagos penguin. Cormorants are dark-colored, long-necked birds which feed on fish that they catch by pursuing them underwater. Members of this family are found nearly all over the world,

This ungainly albatross chick, with its parents, shows little promise of the aerial mastry it will achieve.

but the Galápagos cormorant is the largest. Its outstanding characteristic is that it has completely lost the ability to fly. Presumably, its ancestors made an easy living in the fish-rich western islands of the Galápagos and, as it had practically no enemies on shore, flight was no longer necessary to its survival. The wings gradually atrophied—that is, their development was arrested—until today they are tiny appendages, with a few tattered feathers attached. The Galápagos cormorant does not even use its wings in swimming but relies entirely on the thrust of its powerful webbed feet.

The Galápagos penguin has also lost the power of flight but, unlike the cormorant, it does use its wings to give an extra turn of speed when swimming underwater. Most people associate the penguin family with the icy waters of the Antarctic, but, in remote times, a few traveled northward with the

Humboldt Current, and the Galápagos penguin actually settled right on the equator. Today, small colonies of this rare
bird nest there in cracks and tunnels in the lava. I have found
it fascinating to see these descendants of birds from the cold
waters of the far south swimming alongside tropical iguanas
and brightly-colored coral fish—such a sight is without parallel
in the world.

The archipelago is also the rather unexpected outpost of
another group of birds, the flamingoes. These stately, long-
legged birds live in the few salt-water lagoons that are hidden
in the lava fields just behind the coasts. Their lovely, soft pink
color changes to crimson and black when they take to flight.
Their eggs are laid in mud-pie nests which they build in the
shallow waters of the lagoons.

There are not many mammals in the Galápagos but both fur
seals and sea lions breed there in considerable numbers. The
Galápagos sea lion is closely related to the one found off the

Sea lions on the beach at Santa Fe

coast of California and belongs to the same intelligent species which is trained for circuses. It lives in large, noisy herds on most of the sheltered, sandy beaches of the islands. Each herd has one large bull, who is lord and master of a number of females and youngsters. The young lead a near idyllic life, spending much of their time playing together in shallow pools, chasing crabs and surf-riding in the breakers.

The ancestors of the Galápagos fur seal, like those of the penguin, came from the cool southern seas with the Humboldt Current. It is smaller than the sea lion, with large, liquid eyes and soft underfur—and it is confined more to the rocky and wilder coastlines. During the heat of the day, fur seals come up on shore to doze in caves and beneath overhangs in the lava. This attractive animal was once believed to be extinct, owing to the ruthless way in which it was slaughtered to make fur coats, but, thanks to its protection in recent years, its numbers are now rapidly recovering.

One of the most extraordinary of all Galápagos animals is the marine iguana. This is the only seagoing lizard in the world. Like its distant cousin, the land iguana, it is vegetarian, but, instead of eating cactus, it feeds on seaweed. Divers have seen these lizards over fifty feet below the surface of the water and they can stay under for half an hour at a time. Marine iguanas scull themselves along like newts, with their long, flattened tails. Strong claws help them to clamber over wave-lashed rocks. When it is warm and the tide high, they like to bask in the sun, clustering together in many hundreds on the black rocks just above the surf. They rarely go more than a few yards inland. Although they look like fearsome beasts, they are quite harmless and will not bite when picked up. The adult males grow to be about four feet in length, except those of Isabela, which may occasionally reach even five feet. The young are a charcoal color, but the big males have patches of dull reds and browns. The most impressive, I always think, are those of Española, which have really gaudy splashes of red and turquoise on their sides.

These large herds of dragonlike marine iguanas, the tortoises roaming over the lava, and the weird, volcanic landscapes give a strange and almost fabulous atmosphere to the Galápagos Islands. In many ways, a journey there is like stepping back through time into the Age of Reptiles. Into this remote and peaceful scene, man came in 1535.

3

The Seafaring Bishop

In the Archives of the Indies, at Sevilla in Spain, there is treasured a letter written on the twenty-sixth of April, 1535, by a certain Fray Tomás de Berlanga, fourth Bishop of Panama. It is an interesting document, for it describes to the Emperor Charles V the details of a strange and unexpected voyage of discovery made by the Bishop during a journey to Peru.

Three years after Pizarro had overthrown the Inca Empire, Peru was torn by dissension and troubles between the conquerors, and Fray Tomás was appointed by Emperor Charles to report on conditions there. He left Panama with his retinue in February of 1535. For seven days they sailed with favorable winds to the south . . . and then, on the eighth, a dead calm fell. Caught in the doldrums, and at the mercy of a strong offshore current (the Humboldt), they drifted out into the equatorial waters of the Pacific.

For many days the ship was carried helplessly to the west. Then, toward the middle of March, with water and supplies already running low, the Bishop and his companions sighted land. Drifting nearer, they approached the dark cliffs and desolate shores of—very probably—the island we know today

A nesting frigate bird presides over a blue-footed booby colony.

as Santa Fe. Fray Tomás wrote of the giant tortoises and cacti
he saw, of the iguanas—that reminded him of serpents—of the
stark volcanic scenery, and about his party traveling to a
second and larger island in a desperate search for water. After
a long and difficult journey back to the mainland, the Bishop
sent his report of this unexpected detour, together with details
of the position of the islands he had found, to Emperor
Charles.

   Although Tomás de Berlanga goes down in history as the
discoverer of the Galápagos Islands, his adventure aroused very
special interest at the time in parts of Peru. The Incas had
related to the Spaniards stories of a still stranger voyage that
had been made even before Columbus sailed to the New
World. The Incas had no written language and the story came

37

down as information learned and recounted in turn by successive Inca descendants. It was told to Pedro Sarmiento de Gamboa, the Spanish historian of early Peru, and recorded in his official *History of the Incas* that was sent to Spain in 1572.

Some time between the years 1485 and 1488, Tupac Yupanqui, grandfather of the monarch Atahualpa Inca, brought together twenty thousand men and a great fleet of rafts and sailed off in search of some distant islands that had been reported in the western sea. They were away for nearly a year. When at last they returned, the Incas brought a very strange collection of trophies and the report of finding two islands, Nina-chumbi (Island of Fire) and Hahua-chumbi (Outer Island). Among the trophies, which were later exhibited at the imperial capital of Cuzco, were a Negro slave, gold, and the skin and jawbone of an animal said to be a horse.

Where the Inca Tupac went on his great voyage is, of course, a very open question. Had it been to the Galápagos, it is difficult to think why no more than two islands had been seen. In any event, his trophies could never have come from the Galápagos. He may have visited other islands, more to the southwest, as Gamboa thought, or, judging by the length of time he was away, there may have been several landfalls during the voyage. Yet, even with the strange features of the story, which, like many legends, could have been distorted and muddled with time, it is difficult to rule out entirely the possibility that Tupac Yupanqui was the first man to set eyes on a volcanic eruption in the Galápagos Islands.

The seagoing abilities of the large sailing rafts of the early Peruvians, which could be steered by an ingenious system of centerboards, were ably demonstrated by the Norwegian explorer, Thor Heyerdahl, during his famous voyage on the *Kon-Tiki*. Certainly, the Galápagos were within the range of these native craft. Many, like Heyerdahl, have believed that the Galápagos Islands were visited and used, possibly as a fishing outpost, in pre-Columbian times. Fragments of pottery of an early type have been found in the archipelago. But, unfortunately, the origin of these relics, discovered at campsites used by the buccaneers, remains too uncertain to provide any conclusive evidence one way or the other.

For the better part of three centuries after their discovery, the Galápagos received only occasional or temporary visitors. From time to time, beginning during the sixteenth century, caravels of Spanish adventurers sailed among the islands. Afterward, they became the haunt of British buccaneers who were engaged in piracy and plundering along the Spanish-American coast. The islands offered, in those days, an ideal base. There were good anchorages, calm beaches for scraping

In the seventeenth century, buccaneers came to the hidden and calm beaches of the Galápagos to repair their ships.

and repairing wooden-hulled ships, and an abundance of tortoises for fresh meat. Once the pirates knew the two or three places in the islands where fresh water was located, they could hide away for long periods without any real fear of reprisals. When the mood came over them for more adventure and plunder, to the east lay the rich shipping lanes of the Spanish fleets plying between Peru and Panama.

Among the more renowned of these buccaneers were John Cook, Ambrose Cowley, William Dampier, and Woodes Rogers. Dampier made several long voyages to the archipelago, and in a book he wrote in his later years left many detailed descriptions of the islands and their animal life. Alexander Selkirk, the original castaway of *Robinson Crusoe* fame, accompanied Dampier on one of his voyages—and must have been thankful that chance did not leave him on such barren shores as these.

James Bay and nearby Buccaneer Bay, on the Island of Santiago, were favorite haunts of the buccaneers. Near here they found a place where a little stream of fresh water came down to the shore. Level, open areas, overhung with scattered trees, were evidently—to judge from the quantities of glassware and dishes they managed to break there—ideal for their days of carousing and relaxation. As they came to know the islands better, provisions were made for future visits. Goats were released, pens were built for the tortoises, and, undoubtedly, food and ships' supplies were brought and stored on land. Perhaps the strangest booty the pirates ever carried to the islands was eight tons of quince marmalade. The fabulous age of the buccaneers drew to a close at the beginning of the eighteenth century.

Another adventurous wave of interest in the Galápagos came toward the end of the 1700s, with the growth of the whaling industry. The Pacific fleets of British and New Eng-

The woodlands near James Bay, on the island of Santiago, were well known to the buccaneers. Fragments of their stone jars and dishes can still be found scattered about near here.

land whalers began using the islands as a port-of-call, to take on supplies of tortoises for fresh meat for their long voyages into the southern seas. The archipelago itself had some good whaling grounds, particularly in the cooler waters of the west. In 1793, during a voyage in *H.M.S. Rattler* on behalf of British whaling firms, Captain James Colnett saw how well the Galápagos Islands were suited to be a base for whalers— as they had served the buccaneers a century before. From that time on, the numbers of whalers stopping there grew and, apart from the period around 1814, when Captain Porter of the United States Navy was in the vicinity, their activities continued in the islands until the late 1860s.

Captain David Porter, in command of the frigate *Essex*, was one of the most interesting visitors of this period. Following the War of 1812, he rounded Cape Horn with the intention of clearing the British whaling fleet from the Pacific, an undertaking he accomplished with remarkable success. His

41

base for operations was the Galápagos. While there—in-between chasing whalers—Porter found time to record many observations on the wildlife of the islands. Among these, he noted the differences between the tortoises of the various islands—a feature that was later to impress Darwin and many distinguished scientific visitors. Porter went on to be commander in chief of the Mexican Navy during that country's war of independence with Spain, and, toward the end of his varied life, he became United States Minister at Constantinople.

Several of the earlier visitors mentioned having seen volcanic activity during their stay in the Galápagos Islands. Captain Morrell's description of a spectacular eruption of Fernan-

The giant tortoises which gave their name to the islands were slaughtered in hundreds of thousands by the early visitors.

dina is of particular interest in view of the subsequent violent history of the island.

On a dark February night in 1825, the *Tartar*, a sealing schooner captained by Benjamin Morrell, lay quietly at anchor in Banks Bay, a few miles to the northeast of Fernandina. Suddenly, at about two A.M., there was a terrific explosion. It could only be equalled, Captain Morrell wrote, to the sound of "ten thousand thunders bursting upon the air at once." The sky became a blaze of light, and flames shot high above the summit of the volcano. Rivers of molten lava poured down the mountain and into the sea. The position of the schooner became perilous, for there was no wind and the temperature was rising alarmingly. It was not until the following day, when the heat had grown so intense that pitch melted from the ship's seams and tar dripped from the rigging, that Morrell was able to take advantage of a light wind to escape. As the *Tartar* passed through the channel between Fernandina and Isabela the temperature on deck rose to 147 degrees.

To many early voyagers, the Galápagos came to be known as *Las Islas Encantadas*, the Enchanted Isles. Because of the calms and unpredictable currents, it is not surprising that, in the days of sailing ships, the islands were frequently hard to find. What was perhaps more disturbing was that vessels could often only leave again after many delays and difficulties, so helplessly were they at the mercy of the currents. Low sea mists added further to the reputation of islands that they were bewitched, and could disappear and reappear at will. From their early visitors, the islands received sets of Spanish and English names. But in the absence of reliable maps, it was often difficult, if not impossible, for later voyagers to know to which island a particular name referred. One of the ways that was found to get around this problem was the simple, but not very useful, idea of giving an island yet another name. As a

Flightless cormorants under the noonday sun on Fernandina. Many stories were woven by the early navigators about the mysterious Enchanted Isles and their strange wildlife.

Letters posted in this white-painted barrel, labeled "Galápagos Post Office," are picked up by passing yachts today and speeded on to their destinations, following the unbroken custom started by the whaling ships back in the eighteenth century.

result, many came to have three or more names—and at least one (Santa Cruz) was given eight!

The first map to include the archipelago was published in 1570, but it was not until 1835, and the visit of Captain Robert FitzRoy on the *Beagle,* that a detailed navigational chart of the islands was drawn up. Before 1835, maps had shown the Galápagos in a variety of artistic ways that did little to make navigation in the treacherous currents safer. In 1892, four hundred years after Columbus' momentous discovery of the New World, the islands were renamed *Archipiélago de Colón,* in honor of the great navigator. Today, both locally in Ecuador and overseas, the name "Galápagos" is more widely preferred and used. *Galápago* is the Spanish word for tortoise, those extraordinary inhabitants that have so impressed visitors ever since the islands were discovered.

On the north coast of the island of Floreana, there is a lonely and beautiful bay with calm waters and a long, sandy beach fringed with mangroves. Here a path goes inland to one of the strangest post offices in the world. As long ago as the eighteenth century, when there was no settlement in the islands, whaling ships would come to this bay to post the letters of their crews in a barrel set up on a post by the shore. The captains of homeward-bound whalers carried whatever mail they found to their home port, from whence ways were found to see that the letters eventually reached their destinations. A white-painted barrel, bearing the name "Galápagos Post Office," still stands at this spot. Yachts passing through the Galápagos collect the mail, which is accepted free of charge at post offices in Guayaquil (on the Ecuadorian mainland) and in other Pacific ports, and so this tradition of whaling ships of the past is kept alive.

The first inhabitant to settle in the Galápagos came in about 1807. His name was Patrick Watkins, an Irishman who had been a crew member of a British ship and was put ashore at Floreana. Whether he was left behind at his own wish, or at that of his captain, was not recorded. He seems to have been a wild and resourceful character, somehow acquiring some seeds and dividing his efforts between growing potatoes and pumpkins and, in turn, procuring rum. Vegetables were taken down from his hut in the hills for the passing whale ships, either to be sold directly or, more simply, exchanged for liquor. In time, he gathered around him a few companions whom he treated as slaves. After six or seven years on the island, he made his way to Guayaquil in a stolen boat.

During all this time, no country had taken formal possession of the Galápagos. Spain could be considered as having certain claims, at least in theory, under the celebrated Bull of 1493, in which Pope Alexander VI divided up the New World in favor of the Catholic kings. But the Spanish government had never had cause to exert this claim, far less maintain a garrison on the islands.

After the dissolution of the Spanish-American Empire, General José Villamil proposed to the government of Ecuador a scheme for the colonization of the Galápagos. In October of 1831, a mission was sent to report on the prospects for gathering archil, a lichen that grew abundantly in the archipelago and was used in the dye industry. Early in the next year, the first President of Ecuador, General Juan José Flores, authorized Colonel Ignacio Hernandez to be sent to take over the islands as a territorial possession. The ceremony was held on February 12, 1832, on Floreana, before the hastily assembled and no doubt surprised crews of several whalers that happened to be at anchor in the bay.

That same year, the first settlement was established on Floreana by General Villamil. Land was cleared in the highlands for farming and fruit plantations and, for a few years,

46

The first inhabitants of the Galápagos settled in the highlands of Floreana. Clearings, today, are farmed by a handful of families living on the island.

the little colony prospered. When the government of Ecuador made it a convict settlement, troubles began and it had to be abandoned.

Not many years later, history repeated itself. A new settlement was founded and, after receiving its consignment of convicts, also failed.

In 1869, Manuel Cobos and José Monroy sailed from Guayaquil to found the colony of Progreso, in the south of San Cristóbal. Cobos was a man of prodigious energy and within twenty years he had developed the high volcanic terrain into one of the largest sugar plantations of Ecuador. In addition, Progreso became a center for archil gathering, cattle raising, fruit and coffee growing, the bulk of the produce being sent to mainland markets. In terms of organization and production,

47

the colony enjoyed a success that has hardly been equaled since, but the venture was a far from happy one. Cobos, besides his remarkable business ability, appears to have been a man who was cruel and treated his workers with an intolerable harshness. In 1904, they rose up and killed him.

In spite of further tragedies and privations, however, the colony continued and grew, receiving new settlers from Ambato and other Andean regions of Ecuador. The port of access on the coast, Puerto Baquerizo Moreno, is today the administrative center of the archipelago.

In 1895, the Intendant of Guayaquil, Don Antonio Gil, gathered together a number of vagrants from the streets of Guayaquil and embarked them on the sloop *Tomasita* to

colonize Isabela. Eighty persons arrived and settled on the southern slope of the great volcano of Sierra Negra. By the turn of the century, two hundred colonists were established there, earning a living mainly by raising cattle and exporting sulfur, seal skins, and tortoise oil to the continent.

Before 1846, several crude homes of archil gatherers had been built at Whale Bay, on the west coast of Santa Cruz. From there, a trail went inland to the little groves of orange and lemon trees that had been planted—possibly, it is said, by pirates—at Santa Rosa and Salasaca. Finally abandoned, these huts survived until the end of the nineteenth century.

No real attempt was made to inhabit Santa Cruz, however, until the arrival of a Norwegian colonizing expedition in 1926.

Mangrove and beach at Tortuga Bay on Santa Cruz

The initial years were the usual tale of frustration and disunity for the new settlers, added to frequent shortages of water and other bare necessities of life. Many returned to their native Norway, but a few remained. These were joined by families and wanderers from the Ecuadorian mainland and from overseas. All came, for one reason or another, to seek a new life in the harsh and bizarre surroundings of the Galápagos.

No more tragic or stranger figure passes through the pages of this period of Galápagos history than that of the Baroness Eloïse Bosquet de Wagner-Wehrborn. Arriving in 1932—supposedly from Austria—she settled on Floreana with two companions and proclaimed herself Empress of the Galápagos. From time to time over the next two years visitors to Floreana came away with stories of the mistrust and tension that had grown between the baroness and two German families also living on the island. Then, in 1934, events came to a swift climax with the deaths of several of the principal actors in the drama and the disappearance of the baroness. To this day, among the settlers of the islands, many stories are woven around the fate and tragedy of the mysterious baroness.

During this period of colonization there was an awakening interest in the islands. The strange plants and animals living there, and how they had reached these remote oceanic islands, had intrigued many visitors, but it was not until the new age of scientific inquiry and exploration that the importance of the archipelago became established in the eyes of the outside world. The era of scientific interest began with the visit of *H.M.S. Beagle* to the islands, in 1835.

4

Showcase of Evolution

At Puerto Baquerizo Moreno, on the island of San Cristóbal, looking toward the west and the distant heights of the archipelago, there is a bust of Charles Darwin. Beneath is an inscription commemorating his visit during the famous voyage of the *Beagle*. It was his studies of the animals of the Galápagos that first led Darwin to the idea of the evolution of life on this planet.

In September of 1835, the small, three-masted bark, under the command of Captain Robert FitzRoy, sailed into Galápagos waters. She was on a commission of the British admiralty, sailing on a five-year surveying voyage around the world. On board, as unpaid naturalist on the expedition, was young Charles Darwin. During the five weeks they spent in the islands, FitzRoy charted the main anchorages and their approaches, while Darwin spent all the time he could on land, adding to his collections of plants and rocks, insects and birds.

Over the previous three years, as the *Beagle* had worked her way around the coasts of Patagonia, visiting the Falkland Islands and Tierra del Fuego, Darwin had learned a great deal about the geology and wildlife of South America. What impressed him when he came to the Galápagos were the many curious features of the plants and animals. They were basically the same as others he had seen before on the voyage, in that they were tortoises, iguanas, finches, cacti and so on, but they were all different from their mainland relatives in certain distinctive ways. At the same time, an overwhelming feature of the islands was the abundant evidence of their volcanic history. Wherever Darwin went on shore, there were cones, craters, and lava fields, some obviously very fresh. In geological terms, the islands appeared to be new. Later, as he came to think over these facts, the naturalist grew more and more convinced that life could not always have been there. Colonists must have arrived at a not so very distant time in the past, and, in these harsh and isolated islands, they had become modified in the various ways he had noted.

Darwin made another puzzling discovery—that species even differed from island to island. The vice-governor of the archipelago had declared that he could tell apart the tortoises from the different islands. They varied not only in size, but in their shape and, in some cases, even in the color of their shells. There were similar trends among the mockingbirds, the marine iguanas, and many of the plants. It was as if the archipelago were a world in miniature, whose different lands had their own distinctive inhabitants. "I never dreamed," Darwin wrote, "that islands about fifty or sixty miles apart would have been differently tenanted."

Perhaps the most extraordinary inhabitants to Darwin were the small, drab finches of the islands. As noted, there was variation in the size and shape of their beaks. Yet they were otherwise remarkably similar. Their closeness in plumage, song, and many aspects of their behavior left little doubt of their having a common ancestor. There was something very significant, the scientist reasoned, in both their differences and their similarities. Seemingly, the same species was represented

Cacti are among the very few plants that can survive on the parched lava slabs of the coast of Fernandina.

by different forms in different places. Somehow, in the Galápagos, he had been brought face to face with the reality of life, with the "appearance of new beings on this earth. . . . Seeing this gradation and diversity of structure in one small, intimately related group of birds, one might really fancy that from an original paucity of birds in this archipelago, one species had been taken and modified for different ends." It took Darwin some time to accept fully the only convincing explanation, that life there could not have been created and remained unchanged. In other words, these plants and animals had evolved—and, presumably, they were still evolving.

The genius of Darwin was to trace the steps that led to these evolutionary changes. Perhaps nowhere, as it happened, could this have been more clearly seen and demonstrated than in the Galápagos Islands. The key lay in the several hundreds of miles of ocean that separated the islands from the mainland. This distance had always placed severe limitations on the number of chance colonists drifting in from overseas. Moreover, the harshness of the country made it necessary for the

In the struggle for existence, the ancestors of the marine iguanas took to the sea in search of their food. Today, these lizards are found all around the Galápagos shores. The trees in the background are mangroves.

few successful invaders very quickly to set about exploring new ways of finding food. As their numbers grew, however, so the competition became keener, and, in this struggle for existence, it was obviously those that were best adapted to survive who were going to pull through. The conditions of life simply worked against the weaker and less efficient, and they died out.

Living things do not reproduce themselves exactly. There are always small, often hardly perceptible variations. These changes, or mutations, bring slight new features, or they may emphasize traits already present. At the same time, the environment of a plant or animal is continually changing. Volcanic eruptions have swept and reswept across the face of the Galápagos, and, together with wind and wave, they have been continually altering conditions for life in the islands. Sometimes, these structural changes have helped with the distribution of a species, while, at other times, they may have split and isolated a population into subgroups. However it may arise, each little group tends to go its own way, adapting to the conditions it encounters.

After he had returned to his home in England at the end of the voyage, Darwin patiently and methodically collected data to support his ideas on the evolution of species. Finally, in 1858, over twenty years after he had his first tentative thoughts on the differences between the Galápagos finches, he joined with Alfred Russel Wallace in presenting their famous paper on the theory of evolution in nature. This was followed by the publication of Darwin's classic work, *On the Origin of Species*.

Ever since the *Beagle's* voyage, many eminent scientists have visited the archipelago. Lord Rothschild sent expeditions to collect specimens for his museum at Tring, in England. One of the most thorough biological surveys of the islands was undertaken by the California Academy of Sciences, under the leadership of the ardent explorer and collector, Rollo Beck, in 1905-06. Many new discoveries were made and important collections were brought back for study by specialists. Other expeditions followed: the Norwegian Zoological Expedition, led by Alf Wollebaek, in 1924; two by William Beebe, in 1923 and 1925; the scientific cruises of Allan Hancock between 1928 and 1935; those of Vincent Astor and Templeton Crocker in the 1930s.

In 1959, a new scientific body, the Charles Darwin Foundation for the Galápagos Isles, came into being, and, in 1964, a permanent research station, built by the foundation, was inaugurated in the islands. Later that year, I was very fortunate in going to live in the Galápagos as director of this

Laboratory (right) and accommodation buildings of the Charles Darwin Research Station. Beyond are houses of the village of Puerto Ayora.

station, and almost every year since then has seen an increasing number of scientists, of many different nationalities, coming to the islands to study the wildlife, the volcanoes, and the surrounding seas.

The processes of evolution may, of course, be observed anywhere in the world where there is life. But what makes the evidence so compelling in the Galápagos is its simplicity. Few groups of organisms are present, so their relationships can be traced with a clarity that would be impossible in continental areas. Also, as has been explained, the rigors of island life mean that an organism has to adapt itself to exacting conditions if it is to survive. These adaptations show the basic patterns of evolution.

The iguanas, for all their crests and strange appearances, are wonderfully adapted for their lives. If one stands today among the coastal deserts of the Galápagos, one sees conditions very much like those the first iguanas had to face when they came to the islands. Some headed inland to the cactus scrub and slopes of the volcanoes to seek their food. They spread out to lead more or less solitary lives, protecting themselves when it was too hot in burrows and cracks in the lava. Their descendants are the land iguanas.

Another group kept to the tidal region, where competition and a shortage of food forced them more and more into an amphibious way of life. Many times I have sat on a small cliff near my home in the Galápagos to watch the marine iguanas as they returned from their underwater pastures. They swam easily, with their long, rudderlike tails. Strong claws were also of great service to them, for the rocks at that point were not always easy to cross, particularly when waves were breaking. But no matter how rough the sea, these lizards, with a little persistence, always managed to clamber safely ashore.

The biologist in the Galápagos finds himself in the position of a detective who is able to investigate a case with clear-cut clues and a limited number of suspects. The evidence is not confused by too much detail. This simplicity, or rather the absence of many groups, is responsible for another interesting feature of the Galápagos.

Here one has glimpses into ways of life that have long since vanished—or would have been impossible—in most places elsewhere. Giant tortoises could only have survived in an isolated area, away from the competition from mammals and the evolution that has swept over the continental regions of the world. Outside of the Galápagos, these tortoises are found today only in a comparable group of remote islands off the coast of Africa.

The absence of predatory mammals has also allowed certain curious evolutionary trends to survive. Among these is flightlessness in birds. The ancestors of the Galápagos cormorant flew like all other cormorants. But, as indicated previously, in these distant islands, where they evidently found plenty of food nearby, these long-necked, diving birds gradually gave up using their wings. In most other places they could never have survived. The ancestors of the enchanting and

This flightless cormorant, after swimming and feeding off shore, holds its stubby wings out to dry in the sun.

confiding penguins found a safe haven in the Galápagos, as free from terrestrial enemies as the ice-girt islands of the southern seas.

One of the most delightful things about the Galápagos is the tameness of the animals. Every morning, on the veranda of my house, there would gather a hundred or more noisy and impatient finches. They were waiting to be fed, and no sooner had I arrived with a handful of rice, than they perched on my arms and shoulders. For a long time, I allowed lava lizards and a great blue heron to come into the dining room to be fed. The lizards, I did not mind so much, but the heron, which could easily reach onto the table, would help himself rather too often, and finally came into disgrace when one day he flew out over the bay with a fork in his beak! The sea lions are

Small colonies of penguins live in the cooler waters around the western islands. Awkward on land, they swim with a graceful ease.

Great blue heron fishing in a tidepool

always very tame and doze at all hours on the beaches, quite regardless of visitors who might have come along to see them. This lack of fear, besides, of course, being so engaging, makes behavioral studies of these animals very much easier for scientists.

It is possible to sail from one island to another in a few hours, traveling, in effect, to an entirely new community, with its own character and with many of its own inhabitants. Very quickly, almost from the moment of going ashore, numerous small differences will be noticed. The lava lizards are not quite the same, nor are some of the giant painted grasshoppers, the land snails, prickly pears, scalesias, euphorbias, nor even the ants running over the plants. A tour inland will reveal other new features. On a walk of five or six hours from the shore to the rim of one of the great volcanoes, one passes from desert to woodland and, finally, to open grassy country. Each zone has its characteristic species. Even where plants and animals are the same, first one and then another may be dominant. All these reflect some slight local changes, in many cases still far too subtle to be analyzed. As newer and finer techniques are developed, these treasure islands of science will give up more of their secrets to help man in his quest for a greater understanding of life.

A lively, nine-inch lava lizard on the island of Santa Cruz

5

The Gentle Giants

Millions of years ago, giant tortoises were by no means rare in the world. They roamed widely over the continents of America, Europe, and Asia. With the major climatic changes that swept across the earth and increasing competition from other stronger or smarter animals, the majority of these giants gradually disappeared. Only on the Galápagos and on one or two small islands in the Indian Ocean have they survived.

Undoubtedly, early visitors to the Galápagos Islands were amazed at the size and abundance of the tortoises. Fray Tomás de Berlanga wrote to his Emperor in Spain that they were big enough for men to ride on their backs. So numerous were they, a later traveler claimed, that on parts of Isabela it would have been possible to walk simply by stepping from one animal to another.

Tortoises are well adapted to the harsh conditions of the Galápagos. They move with surprising ease over the rough terrain, and, above all, they can survive for long periods without food or water. This latter ability was one of the things that made them so attractive to the crews of early visiting ships. In those days of long voyages under sail, there was no way of preserving fresh meat and food on board. Tortoises could be stowed away between decks and there they conveniently stayed alive for many months until they were required. "No description of stock," wrote Captain Porter, "is so convenient for ships to take to sea as the tortoises of these islands." In time, firsthand accounts of the tasty qualities of tortoises appeared, as a matter of course, in the journals of these early seafarers. The buccaneer William Dampier felt that they were better to eat than any chicken, and Captain Colnett decided that "the fat of these animals when melted down, was equal to fresh butter." Captain Porter was moved to write that "after once tasting the Gallipagos tortoises, every other animal food fell greatly in our estimation."

This young rider has a slow and unsteady journey on the island of Santa Cruz.

The tragic history of the giant tortoises is written in those lines. Ships came in increasing numbers to the quiet anchorages to take on supplies of fresh tortoise meat. "Turpining," as it was known among the whalemen, became a very popular reason for calling at the Galápagos. Tortoises were collected in huge numbers, crews sometimes taking as many as six or seven hundred for a single voyage. At one period, there were over seven hundred vessels in the American whaling fleet, the majority making repeated voyages to the Pacific. To these must be added the whalers of other nations and the sealing fleets, which began visiting the Galápagos early in the 1800s. Tortoise hunting on this scale continued through to the middle of the nineteenth century, which shows how very many of the great creatures there must have been. But, inevitably, the drain on their numbers began to tell. They almost disappeared from first one island and then another. By the end of the century, it was no longer possible to plan on provisioning ships with these reptiles.

Unfortunately, the massacre did not end there. Already several villages had been established in the islands and the sale of tortoise oil had become an important source of income for the inhabitants. The oil hunters went to work inland, in the areas where tortoises had not previously been hunted. The animals in these remote regions had remained unmolested, mainly because of the difficulties ships' crews met in manhandling such cumbersome burdens down to the shore. But for the residents the situation was not the same. There were by now a few trails, and the hunters went up with donkeys to camp by the pools where the tortoises came to drink. Their equipment was simple—a machete or hatchet and a pair of sacks sewn together into a kind of double saddlebag. The tortoises were killed and their fat was carried in the crude saddlebags to the camps, where it was rendered to produce the oil. For a

64

few years this trade flourished, with oil being exported to markets as far afield as Colombia and Peru. Inevitably, it too faded away through overexploitation. The tortoise oil men left behind them several thriving populations of donkeys—and very few tortoises.

As far as is known, there were at one time, fifteen different races or subspecies of tortoise in the Galápagos Islands. Ten of these lived on separate islands, while on Isabela there were (and still are) five distinct races. Each of these five evolved in the isolation of one of the five principal volcanoes that united to form the present-day island.

At the time of Darwin's visit, tortoises were already rare on several of the islands. The Floreana race survived for a few more years before it finally disappeared, and the Santa Fe tortoise lasted until 1853. No tortoise has been seen on Rábida since 1905. Since then, the race of Pinta Island—where individuals are believed to have been surviving into the 1950s—has become extinct. So, four of these extraordinary island tortoises have gone completely.

Tortoises slake their thirst in the warm water at the edge of a geyser lake on the Volcano of Alcedo.

The ten races that certainly survive today are the five of Isabela, together with those of the islands of San Cristóbal, Santa Cruz, Santiago, Pinzón, and Española. Just possibly, one more race—that of Fernandina—still exists. Altogether, there are perhaps between seven and eight thousand tortoises left, but several races are extremely rare. Those of the smaller islands, such as Pinzón and Española, were at one time so reduced in numbers that it was feared they would almost certainly follow the others into extinction. However, thanks to the combined action of the Ecuadorian authorities and conservationists in recent years, this threat has been averted, and the various races are gradually picking up again. More about this work of preservation and what is being done to save the primitive inhabitants of the archipelago will be explained in a later chapter.

Considering the many threats they faced from domestic animals and the loss of habitat to farming, as well as hunting by man, it is perhaps remarkable that as many as ten or eleven races of tortoise have survived until today. This has been due very largely to the ruggedness of their home terrain and to their own increasing rarity. As has been indicated, the rarer they grew, the less hunting became worthwhile, and the oil gatherers eventually drove themselves out of business.

The race of Fernandina—which is known by the scientific name of *phantastica*—is one of the many mysteries of that island. The only tortoise ever seen there was collected in 1906, by Rollo Beck, during the expedition of the California Academy of Sciences. Today, it is preserved in the museum at the Academy. The finding of this animal was totally unexpected, for there had been no records of ships ever calling at Fernandina for tortoises. Since 1957, a number of searches have been made on the island, but no tortoise has put in an appearance. A report, in 1964, of the finding of droppings, encouraged the

The shells of the tortoises vary on different islands. The animal on the right shows clearly the high arch over the neck that distinguishes the "saddle-back."

hope that a population might still survive in one of the wooded strips of vegetation that border lava flows on the southern slope of this great brooding volcano. It is just possible that, in one of these places, a few members of this strange race live on, unknown to the world.

The shell of the lone Fernandina tortoise in California has the shape of a type known as saddle-backed. This type is found on the more arid islands, where it has to rely mainly on cacti and the sparse foliage of shrubs for its food. The front part of the shell is tilted upward to form a sort of saddle, which allows the animal to stretch its neck to a greater height when feeding. Besides having longer necks, the saddle-backs are smaller, they have a thinner shell, and are generally more mobile than their heavier, dome-shaped relatives of the moister islands. In the highlands of Santa Cruz and on the southern volcanoes of Isabela, among the pastures of seasonal herbs and grasses, live colonies of the dome-shaped tortoises.

Among the first things one comes across in tortoise country are broad, well-trodden paths leading off through the undergrowth. These are the tracks made by the tortoises as they wander around in search of food and water. They are especially numerous near clearings with pools of standing water.

Unlike marine turtles (which come up onto the Galápagos beaches to lay their eggs), land tortoises never go into the sea. They are, nevertheless, very fond of fresh water and, whenever they have the chance, spend a good deal of their time half-submerged in pools. This helps them keep a steady temperature and it also makes breathing easier. When they are suspended in the water, tortoises do not have to support their weight in the same way as when on land, and rhythmic movements of the shoulder blades (which are inside a tortoise's rib-cage) draw air easily in and out of the lungs.

The saddle-backs of the smaller and hotter islands seldom have the luxury of standing pools. Instead, they must rely more for the water they need on prickly pears and other food plants. But even during rainless periods, a certain amount of moisture condenses from the mists and collects in little depressions on the rocks. The tortoises lumber along in the mornings, looking for these places to get a drink. The dome-shapes also have to turn to the prickly pears when there is a drought and their pools are dry. At these times, they move down from the cooler slopes to scatter through the cactus forests, foraging on fallen pads and fruits.

When the moist season comes, the adult tortoises congregate in the higher parts of the islands. There, mating takes place. The males make very strange noises at this period, which sound not unlike cattle lowing, and can be heard at surprising distances. They also become rather restless, walking around and fighting a good deal. In these contests, each male reaches as high as he can on his legs and then strikes down with his open mouth onto the head of his opponent. There is much threat and slow-motion sparring but hardly ever is any damage done.

During May and June, as the nesting season approaches, the females move down to the lowlands. The male tortoises do not join in these migrations. They stay behind where it is cooler and greener.

The same nesting areas are used year after year. These are some little way inland, in flat places, where the ground is more or less exposed to the sun. The female tortoise likes to begin digging her nest in the late afternoon. It is a very slow business—even after a few practice runs the evening or two before-

An official of the Galápagos National Park Service checks the weight and measurements of a young tortoise. From three ounces at hatching, the largest animals may reach five hundred pounds.

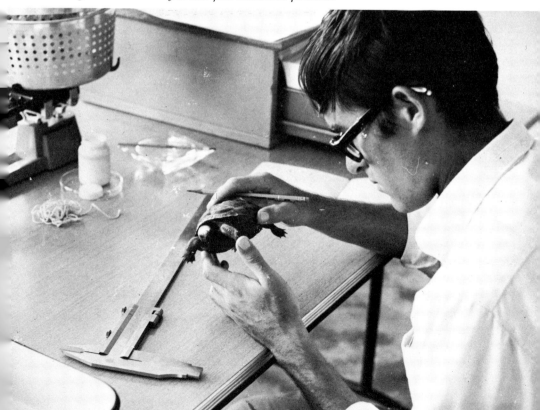

hand. She uses alternate hind-feet to scoop out the soil until there is a nesting hole some eight to twelve inches deep. Usually, from five to twelve eggs are laid, and the female then pushes back the soil and covers up the nest. Incubation is left entirely to the heat of the sun.

Anywhere from three to seven months later (a very variable period, which appears to differ between races and also to change with climatic conditions), the young tortoises emerge from their nests. They are very small, with soft flexible shells, like plastic. It will take many years for them to grow to their full size—perhaps over three thousand times their weight at birth.

There is no reliable way of estimating the age of a tortoise, so we do not know how long they can live. Certainly, they reach great ages—probably more than any other animal. Everything giant tortoises do they do slowly and methodically. They rise gently in the mornings, when the sun has taken the chill off their shells. After grazing and foraging, they spend the hot hours of the day in a comfortable place in the shade. By midafternoon, they are feeding again, ready to settle down in good time in another sheltered spot for the night. Galápagos tortoises, wrote an old Boston sea captain, "are very prudent in taking care of themselves."

6

Man and the Galápagos Today

In many ways, the Galápagos Islands appear to be unsuitable for human settlement. Two-thirds of the land are lava-strewn wastes of thorn scrub and cactus. Rainfall is irregular, and in most years there is some prolonged scarcity of water. Even on the coasts, surrounded by an abundance of marine life, the residents are constantly reminded of the inhospitable nature of the islands. There are few good places to land, and, once that has been achieved, it is never easy to go anywhere. In addition to all this, there come the isolation of the islands and the cost of transporting produce to and from the mainland markets. Herman Melville, the novelist, after a look at the islands in 1841, pronounced them notable for "their emphatic uninhabitableness."

In spite of these difficulties, some three thousand people live in the Galápagos today. The higher parts in the south of several of the islands, which are moister and where the volcanic terrain has formed quite deep layers of soil, are surprisingly fertile. It is here, in these green belts on the upper slopes and folds of the volcanoes, that farming and agriculture have become possible on a limited scale. Altogether, on all the islands, there are about two hundred square miles suitable for cultivation. The area used for rough grazing and pasture-land is rather larger.

The majority of the inhabitants live in villages and on little farms in the south of the islands of San Cristóbal, Santa Cruz, and Isabela. There is a smaller community on Floreana. Each of these islands has an anchorage at a sheltered spot on its southern or western coast. From these, trails lead inland through the cactus and lava to the scattered farming communities, four to fourteen miles away in the hills. The only other island that has had a permanent settlement, dating back to the Second World War, when it served as a United States Air Force base, is Baltra. Today, this is the air terminal for the islands, with a garrison of a few Ecuadorian servicemen and their families. The lower islands have no productive soils and have never been inhabited.

At first, people came to exploit the natural products of the islands. The activities of the archil gatherers, the tortoise hunters, and the sealers were a part of the Galápagos scene until the turn of the twentieth century. With picks and shovels, sulphur was mined in small quantities from the volcano of Sierra Negra and carried by mules twenty miles to the sea. Salt, seal skins, and coral-chalk were also shipped occasionally to the mainland. Gradually, agriculture and fishing grew in importance and, through these, the islanders became, in a certain measure, more self-supporting.

By the early 1890s, under the colonization scheme of Don Manuel Cobos, the plantations at Progreso were producing a thousand tons of sugar annually. Production on a large scale continued for another thirty years, until, following an uprising of the workers and the destruction of much of the machinery, it entered its period of decline. The small amount of sugar cane still grown in the Galápagos is used for making a local drink, called *puro*.

The lowlands are wastelands of lava, cactus, and scrub, totally unsuited for cultivation.

The port on the island of Santa Cruz, with Academy Bay (named after the schooner of the California Expedition of 1905-06) and the Charles Darwin Research Station beyond. Palm trees are not native to the Galápagos.

In place of sugar, coffee production has increased. From plantations on Santa Cruz, Isabela, and San Cristóbal some fifty tons of the dried beans are sent by the islanders each year to Guayaquil. Galápagos coffee, although not of the best quality, has the advantages of keeping a fairly steady price and being stable enough as a product to stand the delays that occur in reaching the market.

A variety of fruits and vegetables can be grown in the islands, but only in small quantities, and these rarely meet local needs. Many of the basic staples, such as potatoes, beans, onions, lentils, rice, and flour, as well as sugar, have to be imported.

Among the fruits that ripen during the warm months are:

74

lemon, guava, papaya, melons, pineapple, naranjillo, and, over a longer season, orange, avocado, and varieties of bananas and cooking plantains. The naranjillo is a yellow, tomatolike fruit, well known in Ecuador. Its pulp is used to make a delicious and refreshing drink. A few mangos, granadillas, loquats, custard apples, date and coconut palms, and tree-tomatoes also grow in the islands, but rarely produce much fruit. All these food plants have been purposely introduced to the Galápagos.

There is a similar pattern with root crops and other introduced food plants. Small quantities grow in variety but they are never regularly available at the ports a few miles away. These include carrot, radish, lettuce, taro (a plant of the arum family, with edible leaves), cucumber, pumpkin, tomato, eggplant, and peppers. The chili now grows in the wild, and its little waxy, red fruits are often a conspicuous sight along the trails bordering farmlands. More readily available, for they travel better on the back of a donkey, are yams, cassava or yucca, and maize. The latter corn grows and ripens at most seasons.

Many other plants, including cotton (which for a short period was exported from Isabela), grapes, and tobacco, have been brought to the islands. Their success has been short-lived, for they are more suited either to temperate or to moist tropical conditions.

Animals, such as cattle, goats, and pigs, which were brought by the settlers and early visitors, now roam wild over many of the islands and provide a living for a handful of hunters. This is, to a certain extent, a seasonal occupation, for during dry times the animals may be too lean to make hunting worthwhile. The hides of cattle are used for harness and saddlery.

In recent years, farmers have been turning more to cattle raising, to provide beef and, to a small extent, milk, butter, and cheese for local needs. With this has grown the need for

Goats, introduced by pirates and early settlers, now live wild on many of the islands. They are a great menace, destroying the vegetation and increasing the danger of soil erosion. Today, hunters keep their numbers in check.

more pastures. Already, the lower reaches of the volcanoes, where the terrain is drier and unsuitable for cultivation, and where remnants of the populations of giant tortoises survive, are being taken over as seasonal grazing lands. The future of cattle raising in the Galápagos is very uncertain, however. One constant problem arises from the periodic droughts. In particular, since the late 1950s, farmers have been suffering from a series of exceptionally dry years.

It is too early to say if there is a general change of climate in the Galápagos, but early settlers to whom I have spoken on Santa Cruz all confirm that mists and rain clouds are now not as frequent over the island as they were in the 1930s. In those early years, people living in the lowlands by the sea planted melons, cucumbers, pumpkins, and even maize after the first warm season rains. Just occasionally, the crops failed, but more often than not, something was produced. Now, in these places, nothing edible is grown by the inhabitants.

Commercial fishing, although by no means developed on a large scale, has much local importance. Some two hundred of the islanders are engaged in fishing, chiefly during the months of October to March. They use small sailboats, the majority of which have been made in the islands. They are powered with motors.

Without fear of being caught in the doldrums, the fishermen are away for two or three weeks at a time, fishing with lines and cut bait. The main part of their catches are the golden, gray, spotted, and brown groupers, and the sea bass. Frequently, mullet, skipjack, wahoo, and Spanish mackerel are taken and, occasionally, shark. As the catches are made, the fishermen go ashore, where there is a beach and anchorage and firewood, to salt and dry the fish. Pelicans get to know these places, gathering around in large numbers whenever they see a likely-looking boat coming in to a landing.

Some 200,000 pounds of salted and dried fish are sent to the mainland each year, for Lent and the Easter festivities, in the springtime. It is a traditional food over these weeks among the Indians who live in villages in the Andes. But the market then drops, and the islanders are unable to compete with the sale of fresh fish on the mainland, which would allow them to continue at sea for the rest of the year. It is unfortunate, too, that the existing Easter market forces the islanders to fish when the groupers are spawning. Reports indicate that inshore catches are, in fact, declining. A closed season, to protect the fish, would seriously affect local fishing, so there is no easy solution. Several attempts have been made to begin a fish-canning industry in the archipelago, but the costs of production have been too high.

Lobster fishing is more important to Ecuador from a national standpoint, for catches are exported from there. This began on a commercial scale in 1960. Four years later, exports of the frozen tails had reached a value of one hundred thousand dollars annually. Three refrigerated vessels with crews from the islands spend most of the year in Galápagos waters, each with divers aboard, who swim down to the caves and crevices where the lobsters hide away during the day. The two main kinds are the spiny lobsters, the red and the blue.

The red lobster is the largest and, in places, it is very common—a hundred or more at times being found together in a single cave. The divers go down to twenty-five feet after these lobsters. They pry them from their crevices and bring them up to waiting skiffs. The blue lobster is more solitary and keeps to shallower waters, three to fifteen feet deep. The slipper lobster, smaller and more slender than the other two, is also collected.

The third form of fishing activity in Galápagos waters is that of the American tuna clippers and Japanese long-line fishermen, who pay for a license to fish in the area. Tuna fishing, for the bluefin, albacore, yellowfin, and bigeye tunas, began in the 1920s and is now an important source of revenue to the Ecuadorian Government. Long-line fishing goes back to the late 1950s. Large refrigeration ships operate off the coasts of Fernandina and Isabela, setting their lines and bringing in large catches of tuna and marlin.

The Galápagos villagers do a certain amount of fishing of their own. The small, shallow inlets are netted for mullet; boys with goggles and spears swim off the reefs to get lobsters; and, occasionally, the red "Sally Lightfoot" crabs are caught for food. At certain times of a full-moon, black slippery shellfish, called chitons, cluster in great numbers on the rocks at low tide, and, on these nights, children, armed with torches and buckets, go along the shores to collect them. These chitons

Villagers net the tidal creeks and sometimes bring in good hauls of mullet.

are then boiled and eaten with lemon and onion as a favorite local dish, known as *ceviche*.

To a large extent, the hardships of living in the Galápagos are balanced by the advantages conferred by the government of Ecuador. The islanders pay no taxes and they are the beneficiaries of a relatively high budget for development and social services. The costs of travel to and from the islands are subsidized. There are free medical clinics and a modern hospital. Post and radio communication offices have been set up on all the inhabited islands, and a school has been provided for each of the main farming communities.

The Galápagos Islands have the status of a province, and the governor, who is normally resident on San Cristóbal, is responsible to the Ecuadorian Minister of Government (Interior). Due to the small population, however, there are differences here from other provinces in the country. The judicial

Lessons in nature conservation are given to schoolchildren on the island of Santa Cruz.

system, for example, is dependent upon the Superior Court of the Guayas Province at Guayaquil.

The seat of administration in the Galápagos is at Puerto

Baquerizo Moreno, on San Cristóbal. There the Navy has its headquarters and the fisheries, police, immigration, and other authorities have their offices. The governor appoints on each of the islands of Santa Cruz and Isabela an official, called the *Teniente Político*, who represents him on the Island Council (*Junta de Mejoras*), together with the priest, port captain, and, usually, one or two elected members of the village. Most matters relating to the islands come before these councils. In Quito, the islanders are represented in the National Congress of Ecuador by a senator, who serves for four years, and by a member in the Chamber of Deputies, elected every two years.

The Galápagos form the province in Ecuador which has the greatest number of schools and teachers per inhabitant. There are nineteen schools, with one teacher for every ten pupils. Among the special lessons taught are those on the natural history of the islands and conservation of the wildlife there.

The children learn the natural history of the islands.

At a senior grade school on Santa Cruz, courses are given to train guides for visitors to the Galápagos National Park.

The main fiestas of the year are on February 12 (Galápagos Day), May 24 (anniversary of the Battle of Pichincha, when, in 1822, the Spanish forces were defeated by General Sucre), August 10 and October 9 (to celebrate the independence, from the Spanish Crown, of the cities of Quito and Guayaquil). On these days, which are public holidays, games and competitions are held in the villages and prizes are given at the end of the day.

The economic future of the Galápagos Islands remains uncertain, as it has been for the past hundred years. No crop or industry has been long-sustained and the two principal sources of revenue today, coffee and fishing, are said to be declining. The islands were at their most productive during the days of the early colonization schemes, when the light volcanic soils were perhaps less impoverished and the large landowners could bring the resources and unity needed to harvest and market crops on a profitable economic scale. For the Galápagos farmer today, living on his small holding or *chacra*, the great problem is that he is not able to produce anything that cannot be produced more cheaply on the mainland, nearer the markets, and without the cost of six hundred miles of ocean transport.

The main hope lies in harnessing the unique qualities and features of the islands—their remoteness, strange scenery, and unique wildlife. To make the Galápagos more accessible, however, and, at the same time, to limit further disturbance to the native plants and animals, requires time and money. That is why the Government of Ecuador has strengthened the organization of the National Park Service and promoted the development of tourism.

7

As a National Park

However prudent the giant tortoises may have been in taking care of themselves, conditions of life, unfortunately, changed quickly for them when man came to the islands. In the Galápagos, in mainland America, throughout the world, the impact of civilization has had far-reaching effects on the plants and animals that evolved on this planet with man. By the beginning of the twentieth century, the influences of man and his domestic animals had become a menacing cloud gathering over the Galápagos scene and its future.

As we have noticed, ruthless hunting brought the tortoise populations to a very low level—with several races even being wiped out altogether. The seals suffered terribly, owing to the demands of the fur trade. Hawks, doves, finches, iguanas, and many other species were collected for one reason or another—very often, simply to enrich museums around the world. Then there came the increasing threats of land clearance and loss of habitat, or fires, and the introduction of more and more plants and animals not native to the islands.

Nothing has been more fatal to the delicate ecological balance of these islands than the importation of alien mammals. Goats quickly adapted to the barren wildness of the

Boobies—"clowns" or "dunces" (from the Spanish word bobo) *of the bird world—are among the many species that attract increasing numbers of visitors to the Galápagos. This is the blue-footed booby, which nests in large colonies on some of the smaller islands.*

Galápagos, roaming and foraging for the scant food available far more efficiently than the hardy, but slow, reptilian inhabitants. Only occasionally, during the early years of their introduction, were the goats shot in any numbers. So they multiplied and, in time, were taken and spread to other islands

84

by the settlers and thoughtless visitors. Between them, goats and wild-running donkeys—with the help of man—have been devastating the natural vegetation of very many of the low-lying areas of the archipelago. Where their browsing is causing the disappearance of the prickly pears, the tortoises are left without their staple food during the dry months.

Other harmful introductions have been black rats, dogs, cats, and pigs, all of which roam in a wild state on many of the islands. Rats must have found their own way ashore from some of the old sailing ships. Already, they have eliminated the more timid native rodents from all but two or three of their original islands. Pigs destroy the nests and young of the tortoises, iguanas, and ground-nesting birds. Introduced plants, such as the guava, have followed similar patterns in eliminating native species.

Through the early and middle years of the twentieth century, the decline and impoverishment of the Galápagos continued. As new settlers came to the islands, inevitably, more land was required for livestock and cultivation. From time to time, scientific expeditions returned with dismal stories of the threats facing the giant tortoises and the other unique life of the islands.

By the mid 1930s, the importance of preserving the wild-life of the Galápagos was beginning to be realized by more and more people. With the centenary of Darwin's visit, the Government of Ecuador issued a farsighted decree to protect the endangered species and to set aside certain islands as permanent reserves. Unfortunately, as the practical means did not exist at the time for enforcing these excellent laws, not a great deal was achieved for quite a while.

In 1958, during the Darwin-Wallace Centenary Celebrations, the interest of the scientific world again turned to the Galápagos Islands. Recent reports of the plight of the wildlife

85

there offered little hope, and, at various meetings in Europe and North and South America, it was decided that concerted international help and the establishment of a permanent biological station in the islands would be the only ways likely to stem the decline. The following year, the Charles Darwin Foundation came into being, under the auspices of the United Nations Educational, Scientific and Cultural Organization and the International Union for the Conservation of Nature and Natural Resources. Under the presidency of Professor Victor van Straelen of Belgium and with its headquarters in Brussels, the foundation was entrusted by the Government of Ecuador with the establishment and organization of a research station, the Charles Darwin Research Station, having programs to promote the study and preservation of the flora and fauna of the

Visitors at the Tortoise Rearing House on the Station. This specially-designed building was completed in 1970 to house incubators and rearing pens for the threatened races of tortoises.

islands. At the same time, the government of Ecuador brought in strict protection laws and declared all uninhabited areas as forming territory of the National Park of the Galápagos.

The new national park inherited many problems. But a start has been made in stabilizing conditions and limiting the arrival of new settlers there. Surveys of the status of the more threatened species were undertaken and, fairly quickly, a coherent picture came into view of the problems and dangers involved. Work, for example, by the resident staff and scientists at the station, showed that, while populations of a thousand or more tortoises still lived on Santa Cruz and Isabela, those of the other islands were very rare indeed. As a result, wardens were appointed and programs were brought forward to control the worst of the introduced animals, in order to help the dwindling native wildlife. Today, with support given by the World Wildlife Fund, and many other organizations and individuals, this work continues. Under competent officials of Ecuador's National Parks Service and with the guidance of the Charles Darwin Foundation, new emphasis is being given to restoring conditions as naturally as they now can be in the islands.

While much remains to be done and many of the basic threats still continue, there have been some notable achievements. From a few surviving remnants, the fur seals have picked up to the point where they are no longer considered to be in danger. Tortoises have been rigorously protected and young of the most seriously threatened races (of Española, Pinzón, and San Cristóbal) have been successfully raised at a new Tortoise Center, set up at the research station on the island of Santa Cruz. In 1970, the first of these young tortoises were released to help swell the depleted stocks on their native islands.

Each year, there has been an increase in the number of

visitors to the National Park of the Galápagos. There are now scheduled air services to Baltra and cruises around the islands, conducted by qualified naturalists. Tourism is bringing a new way of life to the residents of the Galápagos and, at the same time, more and more people are beginning to see and appreciate the importance of guarding the natural resources of the islands. Too many visitors can, of course, bring their own peculiar dangers, particularly in disturbance to nesting colonies of birds, and so tours are being limited and carefully controlled by the National Park staff.

As modern man takes more and more to town life, so the importance of wilderness areas increases. National parks have been set up by most governments to protect areas of natural

The young tortoises, separated by island of origin, are reared in pens behind low glass partitions.

Identified by numbers, the tortoises are kept until they are large and strong enough to be released on their native islands. The pens are "landscaped" with cacti and lava.

beauty or scientific importance in their countries. In the framework of world national parks, oceanic islands have a very special place on account of their remoteness and romantic appeal, and because conditions have favored the formation of often very peculiar plants and animals. The Galápagos are outstanding in this respect. For all the threats and changes, the majority remain remarkably intact. One still sees new life in the midst of the wild grandeur of these volcanic islands— and life much as it was before the coming of man.

Index

Page numbers in **boldface** *are those on which illustrations appear*

Roger Perry

was born and has his home at Enfield, in England. During his school years, his interest in animals and wild places took him to some of the more remote parts of Europe—to the Alps, the Pyrenees, and the mountains of Norway. After army service, he entered Christ's College in the University of Cambridge, and graduated in zoology. He first traveled in South America during 1957 and 1958, when he joined a group from his university, climbing and studying plants in the Colombian Andes.

After four years in England with the Natural History Unit of the British Broadcasting Corporation, Mr. Perry left on a journey to the forests of the Upper Amazon. In 1964, as a UNESCO specialist in wildlife conservation, he was appointed director of the Charles Darwin Research Station in the Galápagos Islands, former hideaway of pirates and volcanic home of giant tortoises, dragonlike iguanas and other animals found nowhere else on earth. Over the next six years, when he lived in the archipelago, he traveled and worked among the great volcanoes of Isabela and Fernandina and in many other distant parts of the islands that are today still seldom seen by visitors.